SMALL ENOUGH TO STOP THE VIOLENCE?
MUSLIMS, CHRISTIANS, AND JEWS

SMALL ENOUGH
TO STOP THE VIOLENCE?

MUSLIMS, CHRISTIANS, AND JEWS

Margaret Gaines

Cherohala Press
Cleveland, Tennessee

Small Enough to Stop the Violence?
Muslims, Christians, and Jews

Published by Cherohala Press
900 Walker ST NE
Cleveland, TN 37311
USA
email: cptpress@pentecostaltheology.org
website: www.pentecostaltheology.org

Library of Congress Control Number: 2011933495

ISBN-10: 1935931180
ISBN-13: 9781935931188

Margaret Gaines
Church of God Missionary, Educator, and Pastor

TABLE OF CONTENTS

Preface

> I bow my forehead to the dust;
> I veil my eyes for shame,
> And urge, in trembling self-distrust,
> A prayer without a claim.
>
> No offering of mine own I have
> Nor work my faith to prove;
> I can but give the gifts he gave
> And plead his love for love.
> > John Greenleaf Whittier

Has our overestimation of leaders' abilities led to disappointment in the results of their actions? Do we interpret their ability to formulate a plan and articulate it to promoters as proof positive of their wisdom to execute expeditiously with justice and impartiality? Have we underestimated the power of greed, vindictive religious crusaders, or political schemers to divorce God's perfect timing in order to launch themselves as self-appointed prophets to achieve what God's Word foretells? Have we failed to appraise accurately the unintended damages of our impatient distrust of God's proven faithfulness to act 'in the fullness of time'?

When opening the mission in Tunisia, North Africa, I earnestly prayed, 'Lord, do not let me teach trusting students anything they will have to unlearn later. Please help me be an example of what I teach. By all means, Lord, teach my soul to wait on you.' Hence, my 'trembling self-distrust' today. May my God overrule my ignorance and be exalted.

Acknowledgments are due to friends who helped me write this manuscript in the year 2000, when its contents could not have been more controversial. Dr Rickie D. Moore encouraged me to complete it even beyond Chapter 4, which, I suspect, silenced him for a season. He typed and proofread the whole work for which he deserves recognition. Sheila Kitchens, who graciously researched much of my material for me and offered pertinent advice is not forgotten. Dr Mark Roberts of Oral Roberts University took time from his busy schedule to express his recommendations and impressions although he suspected I was 'out of my depth'. I deeply appreciate his advice.

Eleven years of experiences and changes have enlightened the situation in the Middle East. I give these ideas to my readers and invite any inquirers or contenders to feel free to contact me for current responses as we seek to know and to do God's good pleasure.

Margaret Gaines

1

WHAT ROUSED ME

'No! Why?' My indignant outburst surprised me. Characteristically I restrained myself from impulsive reactions. Living as a missionary among Arabs and Jews for forty-four years taught me well to weigh carefully what I heard, to stay informed, and to interpret each situation in the best possible light for all parties involved. Then I should speak as little as I could, except in prayer to God. Therefore, I was alarmed and alerted by my spontaneous cry, 'No! Why?'

What jarred me out of my relaxed state? Why the unpremeditated response? Was this the premonition of something wrong?

The occasion was President Clinton's urging of OPEC to lower oil prices in the summer of 2000. The United States and most of the Western world suffered real pressure from high oil prices. Every sector of society felt the pinch. Maybe the pinch was timely and should have been taken as a gentle wake-up call.

It seems as though this nation has had several alarms piercing its slumber in recent years. Jolted awake, we have done little more than register the immediate disaster, point some accusing fingers, then press the snooze button, snuggle down in our comfort, and doze off again.

And why not? Isn't this America. God bless her, 'the land of the free and the home of the brave'.

God has blessed America super-abundantly. This is a land of opportunity where everyone has a chance to do well if he or she, even without a strong body, has a sound mind and a determination to work. Immigrants from various nations, arriving with deep appreciation of the chance to work without molestation, joined our law-abiding, conscientious workers to prove that fact.

A strong work ethic with modest lifestyles characterizes these productive, contented immigrants.

Then why the premonition of something wrong? What are the unheeded alerts? There has to be alarm when televised political debates and talk shows reveal a rage that goes beyond mere discontentment. They range from the polite, self-controlled discussions to outright obscene belligerence, without finding solutions.

It is alarming when confessed murderers offer the reason, 'I just wanted to do it'.

What an alarm it is when children who have everything they ever desired steal something they already have! When asked, 'Why did you steal it?' They answer, 'I wanted it.' What is the unidentified emptiness in that child's life that produces such senseless felonies? It reminds me of times in my life when I would eat to my fill of a variety of foods yet felt hungry for something I could not identify. What is their unsatisfied want?

Is it not an alarm when children from affluent homes murder their family members because they could not do as they pleased?

It is amazing that teens from 'good homes' where they have been trusted and provided with every modern technological advantage can plan and carry out a murderous attack on their school, killing many. What is the missing factor?

What is the basis for anti-government organizations that wield influence strong enough to prompt a man to feel justified in blowing up a government building, killing hundreds? Is it a symptom of some basic wrong in modem society when a person walks coolly into a workplace, a playground, or a fast food restaurant and randomly kills as many as possible?

Something is drastically wrong, and a more affluent and unrestrained, over-producing and over-consuming society will only increase the problem. I have experienced more contentment and morality under severe economical and political difficulties in other countries where I have lived.

From April 1952 until December 1961, I lived in Tunisia, North Africa. France was governing Tunisia, and most French families had good employment and average to high living standards. Mealtime was especially joyous around a well-set table. Fathers were honored and they showed their loving attention to their wives and children. I was invited on numerous occasions to enjoy fellowship with the happy families.

During that era, Sicilians, Greeks, Maltese, Jews, and Arabs all brought their appealing contributions to this most hospitable country. The Italians' love for the arts and beauty reached down into the barest of homes where jovial *maninas* (mothers) created delicious meals from the cheapest fruits and vegetables available in the open market. Big, contented families with abundant laughter and warmth made each family meeting a celebration, a symphony of love.

One very poor Sicilian family prayed daily for God to supply their food. They had olives, olive oil, and garlic from a grandfather's farm. Rosina, the aunt, who lived with the family, was a good seamstress. Every day she would sew something, at least a pair of shorts for a small boy or occasionally some beautiful garment which brought a better price. Payment for the shorts provided money for Rosina to buy some spaghetti and fifty grams of tomato paste, which the grocer dipped out of a kilogram-sized can, placed on a piece of newspaper, and weighed on a scale against iron weights. He would then twist shut the newspaper and hand it to a happy Rosina, who would go home and cook spaghetti for the family's supper. How joyful they were when we shared the food!

I took a Greek mother of seven to her home on a small farm where she was returning after the birth of her newest baby girl. After a forty-kilometer drive through wheat fields or olive groves, we passed a few kilometers of rugged terrain at the end of which we saw the home. The adobe-style house sat in an enclosure with several olive trees, a lemon tree, one goat, and a few chickens on a bleak hillside with no immediate neighbors. They insisted that I stay for dinner, which consisted of burghul and a soup made of part of a fat sheep tail, one onion, one carrot, and one turnip. With grace and thanksgiving we communed around the table. The rich, satisfying love that was shared made delicate, exotic food unnecessary. It was no wonder that those children, knowing hard work and survival skills, grew up to be fine young men and women.

A poor Jewish family of six girls and one boy lived at Bab Souika next door to our mission. Baya, the loving mother, had great faith that her son would become a medical doctor and her daughters would all marry honorably and raise strong families. I can see her now sitting cross-legged on her straw mat, preparing the most savory *cous cous*, which we all shared with joyful thanks. Baya's prayers were answered in time. Can anyone be surprised?

It was an afternoon in the month of Ramadan. I visited Mohammed, who lived with his wife and children in the Kasbah in Tunis. They had one room in a house of four rooms built around a common courtyard, which all of the four families shared. I found Mohammed's wife very pregnant, sitting on the floor in the courtyard washing clothes. I wondered when I saw the pile of soiled laundry, how this fasting woman could finish washing it all and have time to get her supper cooked before the cannon shot sounded the news that it was dusk, and thus the time for the fasting Muslims to eat. I could not merely look on, so I offered to rinse the clothes and hang them up so she could finish sooner. The clothes line was stretched eight feet above the courtyard. I was very inept at raising the wet garments up to the clothes line, using a long pole. The same pole was used to spread them out neatly. The gleeful children of Mohammed's wife enjoyed watching my efforts. Many times I 'borrowed' her four-year-old, Halima. The tired mother trusted me and welcomed a chance for her daughter to visit her adopted 'auntie'.

After any visit it would be unthinkable that I might leave Mohammed's house without drinking tea. We sat on a rug and made a fire in the small clay, three-horned *kanoon*. The ten grams of tea (measured in a tiny liquor glass) were placed in a pot with one cup of water and seven lumps of sugar. Sitting on the horns of the *kanoon* over red hot charcoals, the tea soon boiled. The first serving was very strong and syrupy sweet. It made me glad that our liquor glasses were only two-thirds full for this first serving. Then another cup of water and seven more lumps of sugar went into the pot. When it boiled, we sipped it slowly and talked with the children. The tea ceremony was not over until we had a third glass of tea. This last cup of water and the sugar produced a weak tea. A few roasted peanuts (pine seeds were used instead of peanuts in more affluent homes) were put into the tiny glass. After sharing this last glass of tea, I could take my leave. Years after I left Tunisia I treasured the pleasant memory of sharing tea and life with this gentle Muslim woman in her modest home.

Tea Ceremony in a Muslim Home, 1957

Experiencing simple joys with all whom I met, followed me to France when I left Tunisia. During my time in France, the experience of carrying laundry to the community wash house amused me. Many ladies from the area met there. The six-foot wide, thirty-foot long conduit of flowing water had a washing ledge on either side. While it was a task carrying the soiled laundry with bars of Fuller's soap to the wash house and returning with the wet clothes in baskets, it provided Madame Guerland and me with interesting shared memories as well as the news of the week.

Madame Guerland was a middle-aged widow whose two children had immigrated to Australia. She agreed to permit me to rent a bedroom in her house and to share meals with her. What a wonderful relationship it was. Besides going to the wash house, we went to the city square for Market Day where stall after stall of fruits, vegetables, cheese, breads, meat, fish, and fowl were offered in colorful displays for the eager shoppers as they mingled with friends or convened with vendors who had come to town from the countryside.

Church was a big part of our lives. Regular services were enriched by visiting evangelists. The great caravan of Gypsy believers was so exciting. Thrilling testimonies of conversions from very sinful pasts, delightful choruses taught to us by their talented musicians, and fiery preachers convinced the very reluctant to surrender their hearts and lives to God. Living in their caravan homes in most modest conditions made the exuberance of these Gypsy Christians contagious.

After two years in France, I was sent to Jordan. April 1, 1964, I arrived in Jerusalem, after driving my Simca 1000 from Troyes, France. So for the next thirty-two years, my life was enriched by the local Christians, Muslims, and Jews. Looking back I cannot tell how much I have learned from these gracious, resilient peoples. I went as a teacher, but I remained as a student. An entire book would not suffice for me to recount the adaptability of those with whom I shared many dangerous, deprived life experiences. They are still gentle, generous, and amazingly happy people, in spite of ongoing political struggle. Aboud village, where I lived and founded a church and school, was recently described by an Israeli reporter from Tel Aviv, Israel Shamir, in his article, 'Olives of Aboud':

> Aboud is one of the prettiest Palestinian villages, strongly reminiscent of Toscana. Its time-mellowed stone houses grow on the gentle hills. Vine climbs up their balconies, leafy fig trees provide shadows to its streets. The prosperity of a well-established village is seen in the spaciousness of the mansions, in the meticulously clean roads. The old men sit in a small and shaded walled enclosure, on the stone benches, as the aldermen of Ithaca gathered by young Telemachus. That is the biblical 'gate of the city' or *diwan*. Kids bring them coffee and fresh fruits. Local people are not the refugees of Gaza and Deheishe; here in a time warp one can see the Holy Land as it should and could be![1]

---

[1] I obtained a copy of this article via email: <shamir-netvision.net.il>.

This is an accurate description. In Aboud visitors could forget that there is a painful conflict, while they encounter the active, peaceful local people. One would never guess that they suffered poverty and neglect at best and outright oppression, too, since the Ottoman Empire. A life of surviving taught them to be thankful for any relief and to be productive.

View of Aboud from a nearby hilltop

When I went to Aboud in April 1964, it was extremely poor. Abu Majid, the patriarch of the Saleh family, told me that often 'one could not find a shilling in the whole of Aboud'. There was no indoor plumbing, no electricity, no paved roads, and only three new houses. The village was still celebrating the recent installation of a pump, which provided water piped up from the valley. Everyone fifty years and older can tell of the days when all water had to be carried up from the valley in jerry cans on their heads. I can remember in my own early days there, the Aboud ladies, not unlike the French, carried their soiled laundry once a week to the valley to wash. They would wash their clothes, spread them on the bushes, hang them to dry, bathe themselves and their children, then fold the clothes, and carry them up the steep path that required forty minutes of climbing to reach the village. Everyone, even eight-year-old Majida, had to help carry water. Some pregnant mothers carried a baby in their arms, a tray of clean clothes on their heads, and a jerry can of water in the other hand. I marvel at how they did it. No wonder that it was real celebration the day water was piped into their homes or that every opening of the faucet brought praise to their lips.

When I moved to Aboud and rented a room, of the three new homes I found, one was built by a mother of five. Her husband immigrated to Venezuela shortly before her last baby was born. In Venezuela, he peddled clothes and household items to villagers around Valencia. Living modestly, he saved much of his earnings to send to his wife. She was very cramped for living space, so she decided to build a house. Men were eager to work from sunrise to sunset, digging the stone out of her building lot using sledge hammers, levers, and thick spikes. Others hand-shaped the stone. Some ground the stone chips into gravel. Some built the house. All were happy to receive five shillings a day (seven shillings equaled one dollar at the time) and their meals. All she needed to buy was sand and cement. Fortunately the construction site was near a pool of water that provided non-potable water for construction, and so Om Saleh only needed to bring water up from the valley for cooking and drinking purposes.

Hard work and faith passes down to each new generation, because it still takes the whole family effort to survive. But the people appreciated education and made great sacrifices to send their children away to schools. When I started a school in the village, the young couples started returning. The government opened a school for girls and added a high school. Abu Majid's son, who wore multiple patches on his clothes, answered mockers by saying, 'Never mind, now I am a *talib* (a word derived from beggar but meaning student), so I can only dress like a beggar, but when I finish my education I will wear better clothes'. Currently, for the record, he now lives in Iowa and has his Master's degree and national certification in respiratory therapy. Continuing the tradition, he is seeing that his three children get a good education.

It is just that kind of determination to 'despise the shame' of poverty and use it as stepping stones for achievement that brought Aboud up to the true descriptions seen in the earlier quote by Israel Shamir.

None of Aboud's present generation has known anything but oppression, poverty, false representation, and occupation. Nevertheless, they wear it all proudly, as Abu Majid's son wore his patches, and refuse to let the adversities deter them from their goals.

All of this relates to the American oil crisis and our demands that the world continue to provide the means for our softness and decadence. Aboud has had no sex scandals, much less crime. Few thefts have been known. Differences are settled mostly by 'men at the gate', as in the Bible (they have no police presence). How is it that episodes of American-style violence do not exist in many other lands, in spite of the fact that they have so few possessions? Should we not realize that the root of our social problems goes back to the industrial revolution when the first mass productions birthed the 'have-it-now-and-pay-later' syndrome. How did we ignore the signs and let the pattern of paying 'in the sweet bye and bye' force us into a system, a speedy treadmill, where consumers are mesmerized by cunning advertisements to buy what they cannot afford, do not need, and would not want otherwise. Are we so afraid that our economy would fail, that a new depression would rock America if we were not to continue the heady balancing act of producing more, consuming more? Have we dared to count the cost in wrecked homes, neglected children (including children who are brought up in excellent day-care systems and thus rarely experiencing a real home), multiple bankruptcies, and general discontent, unrest, and unhappiness. Have we wondered whether the appetite for drugs and senseless murders are not closely related to the desire for real home stability and loving discipline? What did God mean when He spoke by the prophet Malachi in the last two verses of the Old Testament:

Behold, I will send you Elijah, the prophet, before the coming of the great and terrible Day of the LORD; and he shall turn the heart of the fathers to the children and the heart of the children to their fathers, lest I come and smite the earth with a curse (Mal. 4.5-6).

Maybe we should seek to be turned back to one another rather than blocking out and attempting to deny the thunders of the coming curse, such as we do when we demand OPEC to indulge our way of living.

For decades our politicians opted to base our economy on oil in spite of various warnings that it is not a sound policy. Oppression and irregularities since Rockefeller first organized the Standard Oil Company in the 1880's, compounded by frequent allegations of unscrupulous management of oil right down to the present, should have made us wise to the fact that Black Gold, a wonderful natural resource, could, if used with unbridled excess, be turned into a curse every bit as big as that which would come from unrestrained water or electricity. And if the United States continues to squander its chances to find ways to diversify its fuel sources and insists on maintaining its exaggerated dependence on oil, the carefully concealed abuses of the past, exacerbated by current abuses, could unleash the curse with a paralyzing fallout that will start at the top but not leave any citizen of this country unscathed.

Who are we to demand that OPEC lower the price of their oil? If we have the powers and rights to make such demands, should they not be used for some better advantage, such as focusing our power with OPEC toward the goal of improvement of the oil-producing countries, rather than coveting the benefits to indulge our own opulence?

If we do wield power over the oil-producing countries, might that not in itself be a cause for conflict? Would that not be a sort of tyranny? How should the people who smart under the control of foreign power be expected to think or act?

Do we need the lower oil prices to satisfy real needs? Isn't it rather, so that we can continue to maintain a luxurious lifestyle far above that of every nation on earth? Did it ever occur to the people and the government of the United States that we could 'tighten our belt' quite a bit before we would be living on even the European economic level, and this could reduce our dependence on oil and buy back some time to develop alternative fuel. We rationed oil in the Second World War. Our present course could be leading to something exceedingly worse than that war. It may result in drastically increased resentment and terrorism by the disgruntled citizens of any 'oil rich' countries, who suffer exploitation and oppression by the powerful oil companies and by their own rulers, the business partners of OPEC.

The peoples of the 'oil rich' countries frequently live on or far below the poverty line by western standards. International travel and television inadvertently advertises to these peoples the fine amenities of life and whet their desires to obtain at least the basics. Even their college graduates in professional jobs often receive little more than our minimum wage. Their complaint is, 'Why can't we, the people of the land, benefit more from our oil?' They have a right to ask. The West has an obligation to listen.

Maybe we should consider asking some questions ourselves. Did we ever try to listen to why the radical Arabs hate the western nations in general and the United States in particular? I personally wonder why Osama bin Laden was willing to spend his life as a fugitive and exile in order to support terrorism. Maybe someone has already asked him; maybe he answered. I am not informed. Just maybe no one ever cared to ask. Maybe it is easier to believe he was born an evil man. But if other terrorists, notably Menachem Begin, could rise from being a terrorist to receive the Nobel Peace Prize, then perhaps some others could rise above terrorism if the world did not write them off without a chance. I nurtured many an Arab infant through childhood, and I never once saw a baby born to hate, nor did any of those I nurtured ever turn to violence, although they experienced much poverty, war, and oppression. What then happens to turn people into terrorists? Should we not investigate?

Besides a possible increase in terrorism, even here in the United States, there is a very real global warming problem that is threatening to result in disaster for the next generation, if not for our own. The United States contributes to it more than most countries, and again it is primarily because of the excessive use of oil. Oh, some are in outright denial that there is global warming. Some admit to the possibility of global warming but insist that we should not 'over react' but rather give more time to researching the issues. It is evident that European nations are agreed that there is a global warming crisis. Their only disagreement is on the method of solving the problem.

Do we need more research to force us to admit that there really is this global warming? The assessments of recognized groups – Scientists, the National Environment Satellite Data and Information Service, and the National Oceanic and Atmospheric Administration – investigating in three separate realms (on the land, deep into the sea, and high above the earth), should be sufficient to convince us. Comparison of their separate studies has affirmed and established the remarkable agreement of their data. 'In the mouth of two or three witnesses let every word be established' (Deut. 19.15). But, of course, Noah's contemporaries for one hundred twenty years resisted his every warning that a deluge was about to destroy the world. It would have been easy to classify Noah as an eccentric at best, or an unsupportable disturber of the peace. After all, there had never been a deluge before, not even a rainstorm. How could water be falling from the sky, especially in quantities sufficient to destroy every living creature? It was most unlikely. Yet it happened.

Before I could get the oil question out of my mind, some time later, I was watching the second US Presidential candidates' debate between George W. Bush and Al Gore. When Jim Lehrer asked the candidates how they would deal with problems of the Middle East, Vice President Al Gore simply answered, 'I would be for Israel'. Governor George Bush replied, 'I, too, would be for Israel'. How trite and uninformative were their responses! Neither candidate suggested that he would seek dialogue with representatives of the peoples of the land in an effort to understand the real issues.

The *Encyclopedia of Multiculturalism* instructs us on who the Arabs are and why they should be heard.

Arabs emigrated in the late nineteenth and early twentieth century for a number of reasons. Many were Christians who had been exposed to Western ideals and education during the European colonial penetration of Greater Syria since the latter half of the nineteenth century; they were motivated politically and economically to settle in Western countries. Another 'push factor' for leaving their homeland was the hardships imposed upon Arabs by Ottoman rule, including the requirement of military service, provision of clothing for the troops, and heavy taxation. Muslim Arab farmers, on the other hand, came to the United States for purely economic reasons, to escape their mounting financial difficulties?[2]

By 1920 there were well over 100,000 Arabs in the United States. But the 'National Origins Act of 1924 restricted general immigration to two percent of the foreign born who had lived in the United States in 1890. By 1927, this number was cut to an absolute limit of 150,000 yearly, a mere trickle.'[3]

Now we have four generations of Arabs in America besides current immigration. They number in the millions of Christians and Muslims. They, like all Americans, have contributed to the development of this country. They have served in our military; they have become statesmen, or fine doctors or university professors. They are a peaceful, moral, family-oriented, law-abiding, and productive people, who have earned the right to be heard. If they were all terrorists, as the common media stereotype classifies them, this country would be in more danger than when we were threatened with nuclear warfare in the Cold War with Eastern Europe. However, I have been waiting to hear about a serious forum in which the presidential candidates express any interest in what Arab Americans have to say.

What I have heard is my telephone ringing and various inquirers asking me what I know about the real issues. They know I could not have lived for thirty-two years in Israel and founded a mission station – with church and school in the Occupied West

---

[2] 'Arab Americans', in Susan Auerbach (ed.), *Encyclopedia of Multiculturalism* (New York: Marshall Cavendish, 1994), pp. 162-63.

[3] 'Arab Americans', pp. 162-63.

Bank – and remain clueless. I have listened to Arabs without prejudice as they expressed what they believe to be the initial injustices perpetrated against them, continuing even unto the present times. Frankly, I have never documented what I have heard. Neither have I been eager to speak about it to others. I led a school. My duty was to stay focused on educating children and inspiring them to know God and trust Him in all of life's vicissitudes. My reluctance to indulge in political discussions induced many to believe I was 'an American spy, a Jew lover'. Conversely, one Jewish settler probably expressed the opinion of many when he jumped out of his car to retaliate against a stone-thrower and shouted, 'You live with Arabs, you Arab'. I was in the middle. I could hear many positive and negative arguments from both sides. In spite of all the verbal attacks and inhumanities exchanged, nothing was bad enough to convince me that the Jews and Arabs intrinsically hate one another or that they could not live peacefully, as I have observed them doing in both Tunisia, where I resided for ten years,[4] and in the Holy Land today.

Repeatedly I have been pleased to watch while Arabs and Jews have been able to lay aside their fears and hatred and ignore their political differences in response to their innate need to reach out to others in distress. That is both on the 'people' level and on the government level, and this is encouraging.

As the telephone calls continued and increased from all over the United States, I realized that I needed to document any information that I would share. Careless handling of ideas and words plants seeds of error and anger, and perhaps this lies at the core of most historical divisions. I pray to be an instrument of light and peace, not a cause for more detrimental speculations. With that prayer in my heart, I turned to the Internet for facts. What follows are my gleanings from the intimidating amount of available information that I searched.

---

[4] April 1952 – December 1961.

2

THE BASIS FOR ARAB CLAIMS TO PALESTINE

The first complaints I heard from the Arabs were twofold:

1. In 1915, Britain promised the Arabs independence in Palestine in return for the Arabs' help in conquering the Turks in the First World War. However, Britain double-crossed the Arabs in 1917 by making the Balfour Declaration, in which they promised the same land to the Jews.

2. The foreign oil companies exploited Arab oil and left the people in poverty. 'We want the benefits of our oil to "stay in our lands",' they said, 'We are tired of being exploited by the West.'

Therefore my search began for evidence, or the lack thereof, that Britain had promised the Palestinians their independence, and I soon found documentation that goes beyond hearsay. The first was in a publication entitled, 'The, Balfour Declaration: A Watershed in the History of the Zionist Movement' by Nili Kadary.[5] There are several significant points in this document.

Theodore Herzl (1860-1904) had spared no effort in his lifetime to convince the Jews of the Diaspora to return to Palestine and resettle it. But his pleas and efforts were not widely accepted. That was before the British Mandate and before Arab nationalism. It is not surprising that the earlier pleas to return to Palestine were met with Jewish disinterest. The Jews in the main were rich and powerful in their adopted homelands. Their afflu-

---

[5] In *Studies in the History of Zionism*, ed. Yossi Prini and Gila Ansell Brauner. Internet version, esters@jajz-ed.org.il website manager, Esther Carciente; updated June 17, 1997.

ence in the culturally developed European context afforded them almost unlimited opportunities to demonstrate their most remarkable talents. They would have had to be obsessed with missionary zeal to leave such a comfort zone and return to the Holy land. In Palestine they would have had to deal with the ruling Ottoman Turks, who were known as ruthless, cruel oppressors, and they would have had to live in *kibbutzim*, which were primarily agricultural settlements in undeveloped land, part swamp and part desert. What a sacrifice of comfortable living *that* would have entailed!

> The number of Jews who had immigrated to Eretz Yisrael (the Jewish place name of Palestine) was small, although it grew from one thousand per year (1812-1904) to three thousand in the decade 1904-1914. On the eve of the First World War, the Jewish Yishuv in Eretz Israel stood at 85,000 souls.[6]

Starting in 1899, Hertzl's Zionist Organization financed the recruits by the Jewish Settlement Fund. The Keren Kaymet Le Yisrael, better known as the Jewish National Fund was established in 1901 to redeem land in Eretz Yisrael and to prepare it for settlement.

Although there had been seven hundred thousand Arabs in the land for a number of centuries before the Zionist movement convinced and financed the eighty-five thousand Jews to come, there seems to have been no great opposition to the new arrivals from the Arabs. What changed it all? Foreign manipulations were undertaken in the service of selfish foreign interest. I quote:

> The European Powers – Russia, France, Germany and Britain – followed the disintegration of the Ottoman Empire closely from the sidelines during the nineteenth and early twentieth centuries. Each had its own well-defined interests in the Middle East, which formed part of this Empire; Britain's was the strongest for the following reasons: 1. It wished to retain control of the passage to India. 2. It wished to defend the Egyptian hinterland, a country under British control since 1882. The Suez Canal was one of the most important transport

---

[6] Kadary, 'Balfour Declaration', p. 1

routes, and British interest in the land of Israel was part and parcel of its (the Suez Canal's) protection.[7]

It is important to notice that in the early twentieth century the Western powers had no particular interest in developing the land or providing opportunities for the Arabs and Jews who lived there. Britain's motives were clearly to maintain control over Egypt and to get control over Palestine for the purpose of keeping the Suez Canal open for a short route to India, which it also controlled. History recorded that Britain eventually lost control of it all: Egypt, the Suez Canal, Palestine, and even India. The world is not the worse for it. That raises the question of the wisdom and justice of the attempt to *control* from the beginning. Could not cooperation rather than control have achieved as much or more?

The first threat to the Suez Canal had come in 1915 when the Turks attacked the Suez Canal from the Sinai desert. The British quelled that attack, but they believed that in order to protect the eastern bank of the Suez Canal they would need control over the Sinai or at least have a friendly ally controlling it.

> They tried to tempt Hussein, 'the leading figure on the Arabian Peninsula', to join in the rebellion against the Turks and the latter (the Arabs) demanded something in return. Sir Henry MacMahon, the former Military Governor of Egypt, now High Commissioner, sent Hussein a letter in October 1915, known as the MacMahon correspondence. This stated that Britain prepared to recognize Arab independence in the territory between the Mediterranean Sea and the Persian Gulf, with the exception of the area North of Damascus and the Persian Gulf itself. There was no delineation of borders or states. It was more of a 'general' guarantee. The Arabs claimed that the MacMahon letter promised them the land of Israel as part of an independent Arab state, while the British formally denied this and maintained that this territory (the land of Israel) was not included in the area designated.[8]

---

[7] Kadary, 'Balfour Declaration', pp. 1-2

[8] Kadary, 'Balfour Declaration', p. 2.

This raises serious questions for me. If indeed, Britain denied promising the Arabs the entire area from the Mediterranean to the Gulf, then why didn't it make necessary exceptions on the west, namely the Sinai Desert, just as it had carefully done in regions North of Damascus in deference to France, who wished to control Lebanon and Syria, and on the east in deference to oil companies, who wanted to control the oil-rich regions? The reason it would have been unthinkable and totally unacceptable to Hussein, whom Britain was courting, is clear. There was no Amman at the time. In fact, the territory east of the Jordan River and up to the Persian Gulf was mostly desert land inhabited by nomads. Most of the 700,000 Arabs lived in Jaffa, Acca, Nazareth, Nablus, Gaza, Hebron, Bethlehem, Jerusalem, and Jericho. It would have been most illogical for Britain to promise to give the Arabs independence in the desert beyond the Jordan River at the expense of their leaving the urban centers, which they had occupied for many centuries. Does anyone really think Hussein would have accepted such a proposal?

Also, it is impossible for me to conceive the idea that Britain forgot about the MacMahon Correspondence, insofar as the Sykes-Picot Agreement of 1916, described in the following quote, does not deny it.

> At the height of World War I, before the fate of the Middle East became clear, an agreement was signed in May 1916 between France and Britain, known for its signatures as the Sykes-Picot Agreement! Under the terms of the accord, the two powers agreed to a division of the Middle East into areas of influence. The Arabian Peninsula was designated as an independent state, with Iraq and Syria also being divided between the areas of influence. Part of Eretz Yisrael was to come under French control, part under British, and part under international control. The area between Gaza and Aquaba, including that of Transjordan up to the Persian Gulf, was to come under British rule. While Britain was guaranteed its control from the Mediterranean to the Persian Gulf, it was

not satisfied with the Sykes-Picot Agreement itself and sought an alternative arrangement.[9]

Here again, I question Nili Kadary's assessment of Britain's dissatisfaction with the Sykes-Picot Agreement. The evidence proves that Chaim Weizmann (1874-1952), a brilliant scholar and chemist, was also an avid Zionist with singular vision and missionary zeal to found a Jewish state in Palestine (or Eretz Yisrael, as the Jews would call it). He was a careful politician who prepared his moves subtly to advance the Zionist cause, which was very unpopular in Britain. To make Zionism tolerable, if not palatable, to the British, Weizmann projected the idea of 'synthetic Zionism'.

> From the second Zionist Congress onwards, Weizmann begins to come to the fore of the Zionist movement. He was, for example, one of the opponents to the Uganda proposal. By the Eighth Zionist Congress in 1907, Weizmann was one of the major figures, and his position on 'synthetic Zionism' was adopted, i.e., the combination of practical work in Eretz Yisrael with continued diplomatic activity in Herzl's style. The Eleventh Congress in 1913 – the last before the war – adopted Weizmann and Ussishkin's proposal to establish a Hebrew University in Jerusalem as the pinnacle of Zionist cultural activity.[10]

Weizmann's methods were to get into Palestine as unobtrusively as possible and to work diligently and constantly to create facts on the ground to support the diplomatic activities to advance to an Israeli state. The current Settlement Movement, initiated by Menachem Begin (who also promised to freeze settlement activity in the Camp David peace agreement, which Jimmy Carter sponsored – does anyone remember?!) has the same goal as 'synthetic Zionism'. However, the real truth is that *it is not synthetic at all* but very real. Nor has the Settlement Movement ever been frozen. Rather floodlights are used at night so that work can go on around the clock to 'create as many facts on the

---

[9] Kadary, 'Balfour Declaration', p. 3.

[10] Kadary, 'Balfour Declaration', p. 3.

ground as possible'. What is the correct adjective to describe such actions? How does the world expect the Arabs to remain quiet while it all happens? They know that the two hundred spreading settlements, with their connecting roads in the small Occupied Territory already have begun to turn their towns and villages into isolated islands surrounded by well-armed settlers. Is it surprising that this state of siege compounded by frequent mass punishments would force a general uprising of the Arab populace? Is it correct for 'honest brokers' to insist on them settling down without listening to their complaints? Is it reasonable to expect that Palestinian leaders could control an uprising of the common people without their own willingness? They despair of any giving peace another try, but they know first hand the dreadful alternative.

Maybe Britain never intended to keep her promise to Hussein. Maybe she thought it was a little thing to throw such words around, especially since the Arabs, an extremely patient people, could be appeased even after the Balfour Declaration was published. After all, the Jews were a much more powerful and enterprising people than the Arabs. But one has to put oneself in the place of Hussein and the Palestinians who had endured untold oppression from the Ottoman Empire for four hundred years. The promise of independence to sorely suffering people who had never tasted any kind of power or luxury had to have much more serious connotations than the leaders of the mighty British Empire could ever have guessed. It would have been more humane never to have thrown that life line to a drowning people than to throw it and snatch it away before it could be grabbed.

But what was the Balfour Declaration and how did it come to be? The text itself is brief and reads as follows:

The Foreign Office
November 2nd, 1917
Dear Lord Rothchild,

I have pleasure in conveying to you, on behalf of His Majesty's Government, the following declaration of sympathy with Jewish Zionists aspirations which have been submitted to, and approved by the Cabinet. 'His Majesty's Government views with favor the establishment in Palestine of a national home for the Jewish people, and will use their best endeavors to facilitate the achievement of this object, it being clearly understood that nothing shall be done which may prejudice the civil and religious rights of existing non-Jewish communities in Palestine, or the rights and political status enjoyed by Jews in any other country.' I should be grateful if you would bring this declaration to the knowledge of the Zionists Federation.

Your Sincerely,
Arthur James Balfour[11]

My question is, 'How could Britain, who held power over a world empire and boasted that "the sun never sets on the Union Jack", be lured apparently against her will and better judgment to approve the Balfour Declaration in November 1917, which was barely less than two years since she sent the MacMahon-Hussein, Correspondence (October 1915)?'

Why do I say it was apparently against the will and better judgment of Britain to make the Balfour Declaration? Again I quote from Nili Kadary:

There were several factors weighing heavily against its publication. 1. Many British saw the idea of a Jewish state as absolutely absurd, the product of a far-flung fantasy, totally without value for Britain. 2. The British Foreign Office felt that 'courting' the Jews would disrupt Britain's relations with the Arabs. 3. The growth of the Arab national movement in the Middle East. 4. There were Jewish anti-Zionist groups in Britain who opposed the publication of the Balfour Declaration for fear this would prejudice the status of Jews who were British citizens. 5. For many Britains the issue of Eretz Israel was marginal, in relation to problems raised by the First World War.[12]

---

[11] Quoted from Kadary, 'Balfour Declaration', pp. 3-4.

[12] Kadary, 'Balfour Declaration', p. 4.

If throwing words around could ignite flames of nationalism in a people who for the first time in their lives were allowed to dream, how far reaching would a promise of a national home be in the hearts and minds of World Jewry who possessed untold riches and technological knowledge obtained in their various adopted homelands? But in spite of all opposition it happened! How was it possible? Again I quote Nili Kadary:

> Factors which brought about its ultimate publication were as follows: a. The concerted efforts of Chaim Weizmann, born in the Jewish Pale of Settlement [a region in Russia], a person who ascended to the top echelons of international diplomacy and brought the Jews a victory they had never imagined possible. Weizmann knew how to reach those in highest position using his connections, his own impressive presence, his reputation as a scientist, logical argument ... and his gift of persistence. b. At a critical point in the First World War Britain had asked for support from world Jewry. c. British Forces were about to take Eretz Yisrael and Britain was interested in a friendly Jewish population inhabiting this strategic zone so close to the Suez Canal. d. Lloyd George had become Prime Minister in 1916. As a Protestant, steeped in biblical sources, he was openly sympathetic to Zionism, considering it a national vision and challenge of the first order. Major historians of the era contend that the entire process was actually initiated and engineered by the British to further their political interests in the near East ... including reneging on the Sykes-Picot Agreement ... and simultaneously appearing benevolent to the Zionist cause. e. After the Russian Revolution of February 1917, it was unclear how the new Russian government would relate to the ongoing war. Britain was interested in winning Russian Jewry's support for the Allies. f. Britain's image would not be that of a conquering imperialist power, intent on repressing people, but of one considerate of local nationalist movements, which would also appeal to U.S. President Woodrow Wilson.[13]

---

[13] Kadary, 'Balfour Declaration', p. 4.

I shall try to summarize these arguments in the vernacular. Chaim Weizmann, who avoided advancing Zionism under Turkish rule, bided his time while strengthening his own position through his academic and scientific achievements. He aggressively advanced the cause of a Jewish state, thus winning over Sir Charles Scott, who was an editor of the Manchester Guardian newspaper. Scott then introduced him to Sir Herbert Samuel – a Jewish minister in the British government. The overpowering persuasiveness and undaunted persistence of Chaim Weismann, together with the support that Sir Charles Scott gave him in the media and Sir Herbert Samuel's support in the cabinet, needed nothing more than the religious zealotry of Prime Minister Lloyd George to advance arguments in favor of the Balfour Declaration. Thus again a very few well-positioned, powerful men made it possible for a government to act in violation of its own intentions to the astonishment of so many who still felt the Arabs had been flattened by a steamroller.

But why should I now bring up at all this Arab claim, seeing that the Palestinians, under pressure from their leaders and the Oslo Accords, reluctantly but finally relinquished their claim to seventy-eight percent of the area in question? There is no reason to go back to the MacMahon-Hussein correspondence except to give people of good will the chance to acknowledge that a serious double-crossing, in fact, occurred and to encourage them to try to understand how damaging it was to the victims. History cannot be undone, but it does not have to be denied. Rather, would it not help the present situation if the Arabs could believe the world is really sorry for the grievous error?

3

RELIGIOUS ZEALOTRY?

My introducing the term 'religious zealotry' a couple of paragraphs ago in reference to Lloyd George, prompts me to ask myself if am I throwing words around carelessly. I must admit, in the face of this question, that I need to modify my earlier statement that 'nothing more was needed than the religious zealotry of Prime Minister Lloyd George …' I do not even know the man, nor do I know his eschatological position. I was not even born at the time. Why did I assert such an undocumented opinion? I was undoubtedly reacting to Nili Kadary's words when she described Lloyd George as 'a Protestant, steeped in the biblical sources, he was openly sympathetic to Zionism, considering it a national vision and challenge of the first order'. Yet being convinced and sympathetic, although it may imply zealotry, does not necessarily do so. Therefore, I stand self-corrected. Yet perhaps I made that statement because I, too, am 'a Protestant, steeped in the biblical sources', and initially I was a Zionist without knowing what it meant. Even now I could be classified a zealot, considering I am so engrossed in a sense of God's calling and how I must best fulfill it. The very writing of this book testifies to a sort of zealotry.

It is, nevertheless, the case that even if Prime Minister Lloyd George's convictions did not go beyond sympathetic support, many Protestants since then have definitely become zealots for Zionism. In this regard, fundamentalists have been in the vanguard of all Protestants. Many have inflated their opinions with interpretations, speculations, and prophecies that bear little or no resemblance to the very biblical sources to which they adhere. If their teachings were not so influential and often misleading and provoking, they would be amusing.

In my lifetime numerous books have been written and seminars conducted in which end-time events had been described and dated and the antichrist named – such identifications as Hitler, Mussolini, Stalin, even Henry Kissinger, to name a few. Many of the books are now obsolete, of course, because the timeline of events came and went with no fulfillment and most of the 'antichrists' are dead, without having done what the scriptures say the antichrist will do. Repeatedly, end-time dates have been set but passed with no change. But obsolete prophets, prophecies, and datelines do not deter good men and women of God, who are eager for the return of the Lord Jesus Christ to earth as he promised, to want to obtain and proclaim the right revelation. I fully believe this is all in good faith and that these people are absolutely sure that they understand exactly what is happening now on the human stage and how it is the fulfillment of biblical prophecy. Unfortunately, many past prophets were just as convinced that they were right, but they died and their ideas died with them. The unfortunate result is the fuel it pours on the flames of violence. Specifically in this vein, I have seen the peoples of the land of Palestine antagonized by unkind, provocative statements that they have had to hear.

I recall when Kash and Mary Lou Amburgy brought tour groups to Israel twice a year in the spring and the fall. A certain Rabbi who represented the Israeli Tourism Ministry would customarily visit each tour group on the night of the farewell banquet. He would tell about the State of Israel, give each tour member a beautifully illustrated book and answer questions. Invariably, someone in the group would ask him what were Israel's plans for building the Temple. On more than one occasion he replied, 'If we wait awhile, we will not have to build it. Protestant Americans will build it for us'. Then he advanced five reasons why Israel could not build the Temple before Messiah comes. These reasons were:

> 1. Israel is not a religious state but secular. As such, they are not sold on the idea of a temple, especially if they would

have to pay for it and live with the possibility of animal sacrifices in modern times. (Consider the incredible logistics of it.)

2. The only possible place for Jews to build a temple would be on the Temple Mount, which is currently occupied. Israel cannot destroy existing temples in order to build another one. We have enough enemies without turning the rest of the world against us.

3. The only people who could be responsible to build the Temple would be the priests. At present the priests will not do so much as step their foot on the Temple Mount, because they are all unclean, according to Halacha, the Jewish religious law. Furthermore, there is no established ceremony for cleansing and cannot be until Messiah comes.

4. Unfortunately, Israel is at war with her neighbors and has to be on constant alert. The Temple must be built in a time of peace, as was Solomon's Temple.

5. When Messiah comes he will bring peace and he will cleanse us and direct us in building the Temple.

Another question frequently asked the Rabbi was: 'How will your messiah differ from Jesus Christ?' To this he answered unhesitatingly, 'Our messiah will be a man, not a god'.

But preoccupation with the Temple and the Temple Mount continues. I can scarcely find anyone willing to explain the details of the temple they anticipate. Most seem to use Ezekiel's temple as described in Ezekiel 40-47. But if that be the temple they expect to be constructed imminently, it is hardly possible according to the vast proportions of that temple. The Temple Mount today is approximately a meager ten acres. This could be reconciled with the ultimate fulfilling of prophecy where the present limits of geography need not prevail, but that would be in the millennial reign of Christ.

Most prophetic interpreters seem to agree that end-time events will begin with the 'rapture' of the church (though the pre-millennial timeframe of the second coming of Christ is a matter of dispute). An important facet of this interpretation concerns the seventieth week that Daniel prophesied.

Seventy weeks are determined upon thy people, and upon the holy city, to finish the transgression and to make reconciliation for iniquity, and to bring in everlasting righteousness, and to seal up the vision and prophecy, and to anoint the most Holy (Dan. 9.24).

The seventy weeks are not seventy weeks of days but rather seventy sabbatical weeks or weeks of years, spanning four hundred ninety years. According to Dan. 9.25, the countdown was to begin with the end of the seventy years captivity prophesied by Jeremiah and decreed by Cyrus. From the time the Jews began to return from Babylonian captivity until the time Jesus was crucified seems to fit, in a rather startling way, the timeframe of the first 69 of the 70 weeks of years, as identified in the following verse, Dan. 9.25,

Know, therefore, and understand, that from the going forth of the commandment to restore and to build Jerusalem unto the Messiah the Prince, shall be seven weeks, and three score and two weeks; the street shall be built again, and the wall, even in troublesome times.

This verse points to the notable decree given by King Cyrus of Persia. He was astonished to learn that the Hebrew prophet Isaiah prophesied concerning him by name two hundred years before his birth. Isaiah 44.28 says,

Who saith of Cyrus, He is my shepherd, and shall perform all my pleasure; even saying to Jerusalem, Thou shalt be built; and to the temple, Thy foundation shall be laid.

Pleased and flattered that the 'Lord God of heaven' so designated him, he made the decree according to 2 Chron. 36.22-23,

Now in the first year of Cyrus, king of Persia, that the word of the Lord spoken by the mouth of Jeremiah might be accomplished, the Lord stirred up the spirit of Cyrus, king of Persia, that he made a proclamation throughout all his kingdom, and put it also in writing saying, 'Thus saith Cyrus, king of Persia, all the kingdoms of the earth hath the Lord God of heaven given me; he hath charged me to build him a house in Jerusalem, which is in Judah. Who is there among you of all his people? The Lord, his God, be with him, go up.'

Zerubbabel and Joshua led the first group of returning exiles. Their names and numbers are recorded in Ezra 2. Jews who chose to remain in Persia gave generous offerings for the restorations of the Temple. King Cyrus restored all the Temple vessels that Nebuchadnezzar had taken away.

The Jews arrived in Jerusalem, set up the altar, and restored ancient sacrifices. A year later they actually laid the foundation for the new temple. By this time, however, the realities of the immensity of their goal overwhelmed them. The elders could not avoid the disheartening comparison between their best efforts and the much more elaborate temple of Solomon. So the occasion was bittersweet. The sounds of weeping for Solomon's Temple were mingled with the shouts of joy for the new temple being constructed.

Then adversaries seeking to hinder the work or stop it altogether opposed them, even to the point of sending a slanderous report to Artaxerxes who ordered the work suspended.

Finally under the leadership of the prophets Haggai and Zechariah, about a hundred years later, the Jews started the work again, encouraged because Darius had confirmed the decree of Cyrus and pledged support. He silenced the adversaries and commanded them to provide supplies for the building of the Temple. Ezra 6.7-8 says,

> Let the work of this house of God alone, let the governor of the Jews and the elders of the Jews build this house of God in its place. Moreover, I make a decree what ye shall do to the elders of these Jews for the building of this house of God: that of the king's goods, even of the tribute beyond the river, forthwith, expenses be given to these men, that they be not hindered.

This confirmation of King Cyrus' decree, reinforced with allocations of government supplies to facilitate the building, was recorded in Nehemiah 2. It was 445 BCE, which some scholars take as the actual point from which to start the countdown of the 69 weeks.

The significance of the 69th week to Christians is that the Messiah was to come at that time, and he would be cut off not for himself but for the people. 'After three score and two weeks shall Messiah be cut off, but not for himself …' (Dan. 9.26).

Jesus Christ did come, according to Daniel's prophecy, and He did die for His people and all peoples of the world. Unfortunately, most Jews do not yet believe in the Lord Jesus Christ. And because they have not recognized Him as their Messiah, they must doubt the authenticity of Daniel!

Daniel's prophecy was for the Jewish people. Therefore, it did not include the 'time of the Gentiles' or the church age, which emerged from the crucifixion, resurrection, and ascension of Christ, and the birth of the church at Pentecost with the outpouring of the Holy Spirit. Luke, in chapter 21 of his Gospel, foretells the destruction that would befall Jerusalem in 70 CE.

> And they shall fall by the edge of the sword, and shall be led away captive into all nations and Jerusalem shall be trodden down by the Gentiles, until the time of the Gentiles be fulfilled (Lk. 21.24).

The prophet Jeremiah, who for forty years prophesied the coming of the Babylonian exile, was sorely persecuted by the people, priests, and kings because they simply refused to believe that Solomon's Temple would be burned, Jerusalem destroyed, and the people exiled. Standing on a hill overlooking the smoldering remains of the temple and the ruins of the city, Jeremiah could not rejoice that he had been vindicated by the prophecy's fulfillment. Instead, that great prophet wrote,

> It is because of the Lord's mercies that we are not consumed because his compassions fail not. They are new every morning; great is thy faithfulness. The Lord is my portion, saith my soul: Wherefore will I hope in him (Lam. 3.22-24).

What a declaration of faith for one who saw forty years of ministry go down without results!

That same prophet Jeremiah prophesied the return of the Jews from the Diaspora in the end time. This was not the prophecy of the return of Judah alone from the Babylonian exile. Indeed he prophesied that return and that it would take place after seventy years:

> And this whole land shall be desolation and an horror; and these nations shall serve the king of Babylon seventy years (Jer. 25.11).

But Israel, the northern kingdom, which is often identified in terms of 'the lost tribes of Israel', will be included in the end-time return.

> 'For lo, the days come,' saith the Lord, 'that I will bring again the captivity of my people, Israel and Judah,' saith the Lord; 'and I will cause them to return to the land that I gave to their fathers, and they shall possess it ... Also, for that day is great, so that none is like it, it is even the time of Jacob's troubles but he shall be saved out of it' (Jer. 30. 3, 7).

The Day of Jacob's Trouble is also known as the Day of the Lord and the Great Tribulation. The widespread belief of prophetic interpretation is that the seventieth week of Daniel is the seven years, half of which will be the Great Tribulation. The seventieth week is generally believed to begin soon after the rapture of the church. The antichrist will appear, posing as the Messiah and promising to make peace. The Jews will be deceived by him and believe him to be the Messiah. Jesus said, 'I am come in my Father's name, and ye receive me not; if another shall come in his own same, him will ye receive' (Jn 5.43). The covenant, which the Jews will make with the antichrist, will be broken in the middle of the week or after three and a half years. Then the antichrist, with all the forces of hell behind him, will unleash the Great Tribulation.

Eventually, God will manifest Himself in great power, according to 2 Pet. 3.10-11:

> But the day of the Lord will come as a thief in the night in which the heavens shall pass away with a great noise, and the elements shall melt with fervent heat. The earth also, and the works that are in it, shall all be burned up. Seeing, then, that all these things shall be dissolved, what manner of persons ought ye be in all holy living and godliness.

In summary, if the Jews themselves are not currently addressing the issue of building the Temple, could it not be that the incredible, meddlesome zealotry of the church unwittingly and constantly adds to the cause of violence in the land?

The Lord spoke to Abraham, assuring him that he would inherit the land – even dear old Father Abraham, who had lived in absolute trust in God for many years, remained an alien in the desert without any sign of a first son, despite God's having promised him a great posterity and possession of the land. For the first time Abraham asked, 'Whereby shall I know that I shall inherit it?' (Gen. 13.8). Later, after offering a specified sacrifice, the Scripture says,

> And when the sun was going down, a deep sleep fell upon Abraham and, lo, a horror of great darkness fell upon him. And he said unto Abram, 'Know of a surety that thy seed shall be a sojourner in a land that is not theirs, and shall serve them; and shall afflict them four hundred years; and also that nation, whom they I shall serve, will I judge; and afterward shall they come out with great substance. And thou shalt go to thy fathers in peace; thou shalt be buried in a good old age. But in the fourth generation they shall come here again; for the iniquity of the Amorites is not yet full' (Gen. 15.12-16).

Put yourself in Abraham's place. He left a university town as a rich man and followed the voice of God out to the desert. He obeyed God explicitly, trusting in the promise. Now God is telling him after at least twelve years, 'Be sure I am going to keep my promise to you, Abraham, but you will not live to see it. It will be about five hundred years from now. The reason is *the iniquity of the Amorites is not yet full.*' Just maybe the iniquity of the Gentiles is not yet full, and the church, instead of fulfilling the Lord's last will and testament (which is to go tell every nation, tongue, and people the Good News that God loves them and wants to restore them) is misappropriating their God-given health, knowledge, and wealth to try to force the end before the time. Jesus indicated that when the church finishes this missionary assignment the end will come. Maybe the church should get on with the assignment and leave the matters of the Temple to the Messiah of Israel, the Singular son of Abraham and son of David (Mt. 1.1), who is the rightful heir to the promises, even our own Lord Jesus Christ. Do we even realize what effect the end-time zealotry of the church is having on current events, even on the level of violence?

4

THE STATE OF ISRAEL: GOD'S IDEA OR MAN'S?

It was May 15, 1948 in Anniston, Alabama. The neighborhood was startled by an unusual but not unknown shout, 'Extra! Extra! Read all about it!' The general public did not have television in those days. The era of the communication and information superhighway remained science fiction. Many homes still did not have a radio or telephone. Breaking news was published by printing an 'extra' newspaper. Newspaper carriers, usually boys, burdened with a big bag, heavy with papers, would ride a bicycle equipped with a large basket over the front wheel, delivering newspapers to their regular route. On this bright day in May they delivered an 'extra'.

Any 'extra' excited the readers, some of which would stand around the street discussing the news. The day the 'extra' announced the creation of the state of Israel, my father's interest bordered on the mystical. He bought the paper, read it avidly, then wrote above 'The Anniston Star' these words: 'I believe within twenty years from this day the Lord will come'. Then he folded the paper and put it among his important documents for safe-keeping. Quietly I observed what he did. My spirit and my emotions absorbed a stunning impact from the event. In a maximum of twenty years the Lord would come! A gripping sense of urgency took over my mind. I was already called to the mission field. Certainly, I would need to 'redeem the time'. The news reinforced my commitment to single-minded devotion and obedience to God. The aura emitted by the blessed hope of the soon coming of the Lord Jesus Christ brightened the otherwise dreadful circumstances of that year and remained as an abiding joy, an incentive to be prepared.

Five years later, in Tunisia, North Africa, an American working with the United Nations visited me. His opinion of the State of Israel crashed into my comfortable assurance. Had it been a Tunisian Arab who expressed doubts that God planned and created the State of Israel, I probably would have dismissed his remarks as Arab propaganda, although I never remember the Tunisians discussing Israel. The Arabs and Jews there had a very good community spirit, and while some of my Jewish friends chose to immigrate to Israel at that time, it had nothing to do with political issues with their Arab neighbors. The American's comments merely dented my armor. I registered the disturbing stories he told and pondered them within my heart, but I remained convinced of dispensationalism, the most influential teachings on eschatology in my youth. Israel seemed to fit cozily into the projected schedule of end-time events.

From Tunisia, the 1956 war in Palestine was far removed. Tunisia had its own protracted struggle with France to achieve independence and to establish its state. Our own blockades, battles, and bombings pressured the French and Italian communities to return to Europe. Bourguiba finally rose to power, throwing off the French yoke. He led the people with tolerance and neutrality. The Jewish community there enjoyed security.

Six years later I went to Jordan. The atmosphere changed perceptibly. The word 'Israel' was never spoken. Living in Jerusalem on the Mount of Olives, I sensed a real tension. When a convoy of supply trucks, personnel carriers, and tanker trucks, all heavily armored and escorted by United Nations guards, passed within view in route to the Hebrew University on Mount Scopus, nothing was said, but one could feel the resentment, and some Arabs did bristle at the sight.

I was sent to Jerusalem, Jordan to teach in a day school. The children loved to sing and I taught them a repertoire of motions songs. No wonder I was astonished when they simply clammed up and refused with no explanation to learn one nice song:

Only a boy named David
Only a little sling
Only a boy named David
But he could play and sing
Only a boy named David
Only a babbling brook
Only a boy named David
But five little stones he took
One little stone went in the sling
And the sling went round and round
Yes, one little stone went in the sling
And around and around and around
And around and around and around and around
And one little stone went up in the air
And the giant came tumbling down!

How naive I was! It took me several years and other gleaned information to piece together the reason for even children to be reluctant to learn that song. Their experience was too fresh, their humiliation before the misunderstanding world was too keen, their very real wounds were still too open and raw for them to be eager to sing about David killing the Palestinian giant. The sons of that same David were still fighting Palestinians. Little by little I heard the complaints against Britain and horror stories of the plight of the refugees. Those survivors told their personal experiences of sorrow and loss with incredible intensity.

Then came the Six-Day War in June 1967. The battle was fierce in Jerusalem. Israel was shooting from the Rockefeller Museum across the Jehoshaphat Valley toward the Jordanians who were firing from the Augustus Victoria Hospital on the summit of the Mount of Olives. The Church of God, situated in the crossfire, caught it from both sides. The world was stunned and amazed when Israel won the war in six brief days. The Christian world called it divine intervention. I just wonder how many, or few, people one Jewish man represented when he said, 'God? We are not trusting in God. Our fathers trusted God and He permitted Hitler to exterminate them. Now we trust in our strength and technology.' I chose to believe he was an isolated individual or at best one of a minority of Jews. I fear that was not the case.

After the war, of course, East Jerusalem was no longer in Jordan. The dividing wall was leveled and Arabs and Jews from both sides intermingled. Israelis could visit freely the Temple Mount, Mount of Olives, and the Hebrew University on Mount Scopus. Arabs could return to visit the places where they had lived before 1948 and see their Jewish friends who had been their neighbors. Although there were obvious differences between the Arabs and the Jews, they were bridged with little or no confrontation. And this was before the rubble from the war damage was cleared! It was as though the armies had fought, the political issues remained, but the people interacted positively in spite of it.

After 1967, I encountered another unexpected and disturbing fact. The ultra-Orthodox Jews strongly opposed the State of Israel! Why? They are the very ones I expected to rejoice over Israel's political victory. Did Israel leave God out of the plan, process, and purpose? Well, it was not unprecedented in Israel's long history. In 1 Samuel 8 the sad story is told about Israel demanding a king to rule over them so they could be 'like the nations'. Samuel was old and his sons were corrupt. They stooped to bribery and perverted justice. 1 Samuel 8.6-7 says,

> But the thing displeased Samuel, when they said, 'Give us a king to judge us.' And Samuel prayed unto the Lord. And the Lord said unto Samuel, 'Hearken unto the voice of the people in all that they say unto thee; for they have not rejected thee, but they have rejected me, that I should not reign over them.'

The grief of Samuel only echoed the grief of the Lord Jehovah. Israel had faired well as a theocracy. When the Lord led her out of Egypt she was a nation of shepherds. She left the magnificent Egyptian culture, the ruins of which amaze even the world today. God gave her victory in the wilderness. He showed Himself to be the Lord *Sabaoth*, or Lord of Hosts, every kind of host, from lice to locusts, flies, frogs, plagues, rain, hail, snow, ice, and on and on. Usually the small creatures of the forces of nature baffle the wit and might of humankind. God does not even need to unleash his mighty angelic hosts; these minor troops suffice.

May I insert a story here? Will you bear with me?

During the first Gulf War when Iraq and Iran were in conflict, the leading nations of the world sent fleets of worships to the area. Throughout the threatening confrontation the media maintained continuous reporting. Many people expected that the tension would be too great for the eastern and western blocks and someone – the Russians or the Americans – would misinterpret their own intelligence and react, starting off and unprecedented conflict, World War III, a nuclear war.

On Sunday, after worship service, several of us were enjoying a wonderful meal with our pastor and his family. Not surprisingly conversation centered on the events in the Persian Gulf. I listened without comment long enough for my silence to attract the attention of everyone present. Finally a visiting dignitary from Europe turned to me and asked, 'What do you think about the situation?' I answered, 'I do not believe the trouble in the Persian Gulf to be the hottest news'. Then I explained. While the eyes of the world were on the Middle East, fearful of nuclear war, God was shouting and no one was paying attention. There were swarms of killer bees invading the western United States as well as the Sinai Desert. Great consternation was being reported because no one knew how to deal with the killer bees. God was saying, 'Little man, I am the Lord of Hosts. If you cannot handle my armies of bees, why are you so proudly lined up in battle array in the Gulf? I am He who rules in the kingdoms of men whether you acknowledge me or not.'

It was this Lord of Hosts who, at the time of the wilderness sojourn, brought Israel through the culturally and politically advanced regions of Edom, Moab, and Ammon. It was His mighty power in Joshua that opened a *dry* path miles wide through the Jordan River during the season when it was flooding its banks. In my own days, once during the dry season when the waters were low, there was a baptism in the Jordan River at Jericho where the baptizing pastor had to have anchor ropes hold him and the candidates for baptism, lest they all be carried away by the current. When the Jordan floods its banks, one can scarcely get to the river. Think of what it means for a *dry* path to be made and maintained long enough for the entire company of Israelites to pass through! The Lord Sabaoth did it. He is the Jehovah of Israel.

However, the Lord became grieved. He said, 'They have rejected me'. That was in Samuel's day. Throughout Israel's history, if anyone wants to believe the Old Testament prophets, God's greatest complaint against Israel was her sin of turning away from Him (Isa. 1.2-4; Jer. 2.13; Hos. 1.2). Even so, in spite of the rejection, Jehovah constantly lured Israel back by His prophets (e.g. Hos. 2.4), and when she responded the revivals, deliverances, and blessings of fruitfulness were restored (e.g. Hag. 1.12-13). The wonderful stories of Jehoshaphat, Hezekiah, and Daniel (I cannot name them all) feed my faith and delight my spirit. The Lord of Israel is my Lord, the Shepherd of my soul, my all in all!

So why do the ultra-Orthodox Jews reject the secular state of Israel? Because it is just that, a secular state. They think that the Messiah alone can truly restore the Kingdom of Israel. And they are right, according to Ezek. 22.25-27. The Lord God speaking through the prophet Ezekiel declared the end of the priesthood, temple worship ('remove the diadem'), and the kingdom ('take off the crown') until he comes whose right it is to rule—referring to Jesus the Messiah. He is worthy to be waited for. The spirit of taking matters into one's own hands and not obeying God was evident in Saul, Israel's first king, whom God rejected even after He had chosen him because of his persistent disobedience. 1 Samuel 15.22-23 reads,

> And Samuel said, 'Hath the Lord as great delight in burnt offerings and sacrifices, as in obeying the voice of the Lord? Behold, to obey is better than sacrifice, and to hearken than the fat of rams. For rebellion is as the sin of witchcraft, and stubbornness is as iniquity and idolatry. Because thou hast rejected the word of the Lord, he hath also rejected thee from being king.'

But how did the United States get involved in recognizing the State of Israel? There is a seven-page historical document that addresses this question. It is entitled, 'The United States and the Recognition of Israel'. This document begins with the British White Paper on Palestine, dated May 16, 1936, and it ends with Israel's signature on armistice agreements with Egypt, Lebanon, Jordan, and Syria from February 24 to July 20, 1949.

The British White Paper on Palestine was originally called the MacDonald White Paper. It is extremely significant in that it reveals an attempt by Britain to repair the damages of the past. It essentially nullified the Balfour Declaration and sets a timeframe in which an independent Palestinian State should be established.

The chronology is a record of all official statements, telephone calls, correspondence, and legislature concerning Palestine. It is critical for what it reveals.

1. Tremendous disagreement between the Allies and the United States on the fate of Palestine.

2. Grave differences of opinion within the United States between President Truman and other government officials.

3. Motivation of fear in all government agreements and policies over the communists' greed for control of the oil and desire to have control in the region.

4. Trepidation, vacillation, and hesitation between what President Truman expressed that he wanted to do and what he actually did as the result of persuasion.

It fails for what it excludes:

1. No mention was made of the size of this land or if its water supplies were adequate to sustain unlimited immigration. (It literally means dividing an area as small as New Jersey for the purpose of establishing two sizable nations with nothing like the water sources that New Jersey enjoys.)

2. Faced with this momentous challenge, Truman never expressed a need for Divine guidance nor did he call the nation

to prayer. God was totally left out of the equation. Does that indicate it was man's idea and not God's?[14]

History records the endeavors of many human initiators, who were not acting as agents of God's will or plan – the first sin of Adam and Eve, the rebellious building of the Tower of Babel to keep from being dispersed as God had commanded (Gen. 9.1; 11.4). Abraham's attempt to fulfill God's promise for a son through having Ishmael is just one in a long parade of examples. The marvelous wonder is that, even though Abraham's presumptuous attempt grieved God, instead of manifesting His righteous anger, God showed tender mercies and lovingkindness.

In response to the disobedience of Adam and Eve, God provided clothes, promised them a Savior, and shut them out of Eden to guard against further tragedy. Who would want to bear the risk of eating of the tree of life and living eternally in a world like this? How incredibly sin increased and is to blame for broken and disrupted families, communities, and nations.

God did not level the Tower of Babel in Divine protest (some attest that its remains are there today). God simply confused the language of the tower builders. He did not have to repeat, 'Go and fill the earth'. Maybe each language group thought the rest had gone mad, so they withdrew from them. Any world traveler, missionary, or foreign diplomat experiences daily the continuous difficulties that persist because of Babel.

God allowed Abraham to enjoy Ishmael into his teens. Ishmael was Abraham's pride and great joy. All of Abraham's pent-up fatherly instincts flooded through the barriers and poured out on that lad. God did not even spoil his fun by telling him what he had done that was not in the plan. He knew that the inevitable heartbreak would come all too soon for this venerable old patriarch. And when that time did come and Abraham cried out his despair to God, 'Oh, that Ishmael might live before thee!' The God of all comfort, the compassionate God, reassured

---

[14] These lists represent a summary of 'The United States and the Recognition of Israel: A Chronology Compiled by Raymond H. Geselbracht from *Harry S. Truman and the Founding of Israel* (Westport, CT: Michael T. Benson, 1997).

Abraham that he would be a father to Ishmael. As Gen. 17.20 records,

> And as for Ishmael, I have heard thee: behold, I have blessed him, and will make him fruitful, and will multiply him exceedingly; twelve princes shall he beget and I will make him a great nation.

Every time human beings choose to maneuver outside the will and plan of God, they create perpetual difficulties for themselves and others. Were it not for the mercies of God, who works to minimize the effects of our actions as much as we allow Him, the world would be far more chaotic than it is today.

5

NOT MY FIRST TIME TO BE ROUSED

For weeks Israel warned everyone to prepare an airtight room and carefully seal food and water containers in preparation for a possible chemical attack. Gas masks were provided for all Israelis and for foreigners living in Israel. The public was carefully instructed on how to use the gas mask. Also, Israel provided a radio channel that was to be used only for reports of an impending Scud Missile attack. The population was advised to keep that radio channel open at all times so as to not miss the alert.

All nonessential tourists and foreign residents were advised to leave Israel. Arlene Miller and I were the only Church of God missionaries in the Occupied West Bank. We were advised to leave immediately. Arlene had a temporary residence visa, so she could go anytime. I had permanent residence, so I could not leave without an exit-re-entry visa, for which I made application without delay. Before the visa could be issued, the Gulf War broke out. I was not in Jerusalem at the time but in Aboud village, on the Occupied West Bank. The date was January 1991.

The Arabs were not issued gas masks, nor could they afford the considerable expense of sealing a room and storing food and water supplies. What room would they seal anyway? Most families had only one room, which the extended family shared. The only food they could store was rice, lentils, oil, olives, pasta, flour, sugar, and tea, and that only in limited amounts, given the space available.

With the outbreak of the Gulf War the whole West Bank was clamped under total curfew. No one could leave his or her house or even go out on the balcony without risking being shot. I still wonder how parents, several children, grandparents, and sometimes an unmarried aunt survived in such close quarters for the 42 days of confinement. What self-restraint was required of them in order for three generations of men, women, and children to endure their narrowly restricted space with no privacy!

My situation was so much better. I had two rooms, a small kitchen, and a bath, all of which were sealed. Plenty of nonperishable staples, canned foods, and bottled water filled my cupboards. I had a gas mask, a battery radio, and a good supply of batteries. I felt guilty that I had so much in the midst of the Palestinians who had so little. To complicate the situation further for those whose room had only one or two small windows, thus making it much darker when the door had to be shut, the almost constant downpour of rain increased humidity and aggravated the chill of midwinter.

The special radio channel for Scud attack alerts was quiet except in case of attack. The Israelis were not under curfew, so they could carry their radios and gas masks with them and continue an almost normal life style. Public sealed shelters were available for those away from home. Their food supply was unlimited and their work and social activities kept them partially distracted while under the real threat of extinction.

The attacks came, most of them aimed at Tel Aviv. Launched from the extreme western region of Iraq, the Scud missiles traveled a mere 800 miles in a straight line before reaching points very near downtown Tel Aviv. Aboud village, only 30 miles from Tel Aviv was in the direct path of the Scuds. Its people could see the missiles pass over and later, the Patriot Missiles intercepting them. I heard the radio alert, 'Get into your sealed room and put on your gas mask until we broadcast an all clear'. Then the upbeat music, no doubt designed to counter excess fear and prevent panic, filled the tense waiting time.

After several weeks, I was surprised when someone knocked on my door. A tall, gaunt young man stood there pleading with me to take his wife to the hospital. She had delivered twins in a Jerusalem hospital the day the war broke out, but she was forced to leave the hospital immediately and get back to Aboud. The twins were fine in the care of two grandmothers and an aunt, but the mother developed a kidney blockage with severe complications. Aboud had no resident doctor or clinic. There was little means of transportation. Those going to Ramallah, the nearest town, had to pass more than one roadblock and frequently a body search, to complicate the trip. Often their business in Ramallah was interrupted by an outbreak of violence followed by a curfew called by the Israeli Military or a strike called by protesting Arabs. These thoughts raced through my mind while I watched the young man shivering in the cold and wondered what I could do. I did invite him in, which he accepted unwillingly because of the urgency of his situation. I told him, 'You know we are under total curfew and I cannot leave the house. But if you can get permission from the army for me to take her, I will.' Then he ran to the military station near my house to ask for the permission. They said that they were not authorized to give the permission but that they could allow us to go to Nebi Saleh, the central military post, to get a pass from the captain.

When we arrived at the military post, the gentleman, his wife, his mother, and I had to walk at least four hundred feet up a gravel incline to the door where a crowd of people waited. We were told the captain was not there and would not be expected back for two hours. My heart agreed with my head that there was no way this sick woman could endure the wait.

Before I despaired, a social worker came out of the military post. She was from Bir Zeit where they had a clinic. She told us to go to Bir Zeit and she would follow and meet us there as soon as possible.

When we arrived at the entrance to Bir Zeit the soldiers refused us entry. I pleaded with them to search me, search the car, and search me again when I came back, but they refused. We could do nothing more than wait for the social worker, who soon arrived in an ambulance. She was authorized to take them in the ambulance into Bir Zeit where she promised to take charge of the distressful situation. I returned to Aboud stunned that I, a well known missionary in the Bir Ziet district for almost thirty years, would not be trusted even in an emergency.

Back in my sealed room, I was shaking with consternation. I asked myself, 'What happened to humanity?' Then I asked God, 'What is going on? I know You are in control. There is no doubt that You still rule in the kingdoms of men. Show me, Father, what You would have me do. What should be done?'

With that I turned to Ecclesiastes 3, and I read that familiar passage several times. But my attention was attracted repeatedly to the first part of verse 5: 'A time to cast away stones and a time to gather stones together'. It certainly seemed as though enough stones had been cast away. The world knows that Arabs defy tanks, machine guns, and rifle fire with the act of throwing stones. Television cameras have caught this irrational act in Jerusalem, Bethlehem, Hebron, Ramallah, Nablus, and everywhere in between. What the media would not film are the retaliatory raids the Jewish settlers would make. They would come to Aboud about ten o'clock at night and stay until two in the morning. There would be an organized party of many cars, including an ambulance just in case anyone of them was seriously hurt. They would bring chain saws to cut down the olive trees. They would line up their cars and turn on their lights and dance the *hora* in the street, while they sang loudly and shouted, 'Come out, you dogs. Face us, you cowards.' Then they would hurl stones and break out the windows of every house lining the street. Also, the bus and exposed cars would get stoned. My car window was smashed in two separate raids. To finish their party, they would cut down many olive trees. That was especially surprising, because supposedly these settlers claimed the support of Jehovah and the Scriptures as their right to be in the land at all. Why, then, would they disobey the law of warfare recorded in Deut. 20.19?

> When thou shalt besiege a city a long time, in making war against it to take it, thou shalt not destroy the trees thereof by forcing an axe against them; for thou mayest eat of them, and thou shalt not cut them down (for the tree of the field is man's life) to employ them in the siege.

The Arab adults and the Jewish settlers were not alone in throwing stones. Bored young Arab boys often would lie in wait behind stone walls until some Jewish car would come by. Then with the practice of a shepherd, they would hurl stones at the car. Frequently, the driver of the car would jump out shouting and shooting. The boys would be long gone. Asked once, 'Why do you throw stones at the settlers?' They answered, 'We don't hurt them. It is fun to see what happens, just because we throw stones.'

Margaret's Car Window Smashed in Jewish Retaliation

Whether gleefully, as with the young boys, defensively, as with the adult Arabs, or in retaliation, as with the settlers, I could see that day, as I sat before Ecclesiastes 3, that too many stones had already been cast away. I felt God was saying, 'It is time for gathering up the stones'.

About that time the US Secretary of State, James Baker, came to Israel and met with Prime Minister Shamir. In their discussions on the violence in Israel, James Baker said, 'Maybe we need to adopt some confidence-building measures'. Prime Minister Shamir answered, 'The Arabs need to go to work'.

All of these events churned in my heart and aroused my emotions while I sat, gas mask on, waiting for the delayed 'all clear'. I could not help thinking how the world had misappropriated God's gifts of life, health, and wealth by constructing all the weapons of mass destruction. For the price of one Scud or one Patriot missile a number of 'confidence-building projects' could be completed in Aboud that would save the Arabs from having to make expensive, unproductive trips to Ramallah and get them to work. Perhaps, for the price of all the Scuds and Patriots, every suffering village in the West Bank could have their basic needs met, their hope restored, and opportunities to work. Israel had already reaped a fine profit from the cool peace with Egypt. Maybe daring to meet the enemy face to face with offers of peaceful cooperation would be a less costly defense than the maintenance of a constant alert.

But what were the confidence-building projects I had in mind? They are so basic as not to be believed.

What is more basic than water? Aboud has a spring that has provided water for seven villages. But the Israeli authorities took control of that spring and all other water sources. Most of the water was used for their own purposes – one report said this was eighty percent of the water – and the Arab villages were left with barely enough water to survive. My landlord had a cistern constructed in a time when dynamite could be bought to blast out the stone, building supplies were reasonably priced, and labor was one dollar for a twelve-hour day. Few people have cisterns. Under the imposed Israeli arrangement, water was turned on for the Arab villages for only about 3 hours a week. Families simply could not store up enough water. When the water came on, it was known immediately. Everyone got busy taking baths, washing clothes, cleaning houses, and filling every possible container with water before it was turned off again. Before the water came on again, especially if it was delayed, a stream of mothers came to my landlord to ask for a gallon of water from his cistern. 'We do not want water for any other purpose than to make a cup of tea for our children', they said. But what about baths for the children who had no parks or playgrounds, but played in the stones and sand? At least their dirty legs were dry, and so much of the loose dirt could be wiped off with a dry cloth. I called it 'dry-cleaning the children'. With a damp cloth they wiped off the rest. But what is the confidence-building project that could possibly help the water situation?

Aboud had a pond. From the earliest recorded history, the pond supplemented the local water supply for non-potable purposes, watering livestock, building, or irrigating kitchen gardens, for instance.

In recent years the pond ceased to hold water, thus drying up in the summer months. It is quite possible that some blasting that took place nearby and caused damage to several structures in the area, including our school, cracked the stone bottom of the pond, causing it to leak. In 1991 I envisioned the pond restored. It could be cleaned out and made into a covered cistern, which would store a minimum of two thousand cubic meters of the water that God so generously gives us in the rainy season.

The land surrounding the pool is almost solid stone. Ground up, the stone cleaned out of the cistern could adequately fill in the gaps between the stones to form a natural pavement. Five or more shops could be constructed around the pavement to create a mini-shopping center. Enterprising young men trained as electricians, plumbers, painters, construction workers, and photographers could rent the shops from the community, with profits returning for further maintenance and development. Possibly there could be a shallow wading pool supplied by the cistern, the run off from which could nourish gourd vines or grapes to shade the area. The shops could provide the basic needs of the village, and for other purposes the villagers could go to Ramallah. The available space would inspire young merchants to make the necessary investments, thus putting the Arabs to work and building much hope and confidence.

2. Why not a maternity clinic? Aboud has a small clinic visited twice a week by a doctor. Wednesdays are scheduled for expectant mothers and Fridays for general medicine. The land behind the clinic is adequate to construct a simple maternity clinic. Mothers from several villages nearby see the doctor on Wednesday. They would probably be very happy to give birth in Aboud, too, rather than risking the trip to Ramallah or Jerusalem. Most births are normal. For any emergency there could be a prearranged emergency service in a hospital of one of the cities. Aboud has enough trained nurses for the clinic. Would it not be a confidence-building measure to give them work at home so they would not have to continue to suffer the harrowing daily experience of trying to get to Ramallah to work?

3. What about a nursing home? The Arabs have little social welfare. Charitable organizations are about the only resource for the helpless. I have visited many elderly men and women through the last months of their lives. Some had no children. Others had children but could hardly accommodate an aging parent or aunt who was bedfast. The one or even two-room home made it a hardship indeed. Most of those whom I saw die were eighty to one hundred years old. In their childhood and throughout their lives they had recited the Psalm 23, Psalm 51, and hymns such as, 'Safe in the Arms of Jesus', 'On Christ the Solid Rock I Stand', or 'Nearer My God to Thee', all in Arabic language. They could no longer sing but their still keen minds recited the words as they fell into their final sleep. Most of them, however, lived out their last years alone and bedfast in a cold dark room. In 1991, Kahlil Khoury, who was steward in the Greek Orthodox church, was grieved for the plight of the patriarchs and matriarchs. His family did all they could to help them, but he said to me, 'Sister, the Greek Orthodox Church has a building that could be repaired so we could get these helpless people in one place where it would be easier to take care of them, but we just do not have the funds.' What a dream! It would not have to be elaborate but just a simple place where the elderly could receive constant care. This would be a confidence-building measure, and it would put a few people to work.

I could say more. In 1991 I did say more. A video and a written report of a number of projects still lie in my office. Did those who received copies think or do anything at all? I do not know. I do know that children who attended our school grew up with a vision. They are still young and do not have lots of capital, but they and others have made a difference. With little or no help from outside, they have set up their own businesses. They are working, and their goods and services encourage their people and keep many working. Maybe that is why Arab violence has been practically unknown in Aboud.

6

WHAT IF?

When I was a child I joined other children in a game called 'play like'. Not having any toys, television, or video games, we imagined whole episodes of family life, cops and robbers, Tarzan, cowboys and Indians, and even church. Our vivid imaginations could transform our yard and the woods beyond into any setting for our games.

'What if?' is a sort of pretending. The French say you can put Paris in a bottle with an 'if'. This is true. Likely there is little use to dwell on what might have been, unless by being made aware of missed opportunities we may be more alert now and wiser in the future. So let us begin.

What if John D. Rockefeller, who felt a divine imperative to 'earn money so that he could give it away' could have married philanthropy to the earning process, thus avoiding the damaging excesses that tormented him and his family? As this relates to Arabs and the Middle East oil, I believe it could have happened.

American oil researchers and drillers met the Arab sheiks who knew nothing about oil, its potential for good and evil, or that they were sitting on maybe the richest deposits on the earth. The sheiks could have been influenced for good from the beginning. They were dedicated Muslims and as such were taught from the Koran to be compassionate to those whom they ruled. The Arab expression '*dakheelek*', meaning 'protect me or bring me under your cover', imposed a divine obligation for the one to whom the appeal was addressed, to spare no resources not even life itself to comply honorably. Arab folklore is rich with examples of just such gallantry. The most appealing of all the stories I heard bears repeating here.

An Arab landowner, who had only one son, lived contentedly with his family. One day their peace was challenged by a frightful incident. A young man ran up to his tent pleading, 'Dakheelek, dakheelek, ya saidi!' ('Protect me, protect me, my lord!') The terror-stricken young man, covered with blood, was closely pursued by a mob of angry avengers bent on killing him. The landowner pulled the young man into his tent, then stood to face the violent crowd.

'Give him to us; we will make him pay with his own life. He is a murderer!' the mob shouted.

Holding up his hands to calm the crowd, the landowner knew the situation was grave, but it had to be dealt with rationally. The incident deserved a just hearing. He told the mob as much. 'Besides now, he has pleaded for my protection, and I must do my duty,' he said.

'Your duty!? Do you know he has just murdered your only son?' they informed him. Stunned and silenced, the landlord finally replied, 'All the details have to be investigated, but I would be more dishonorable than he if I were to turn him over to you.' The mob turned away with mixed responses, while the landowner entered his tent to face his son's assailant, who was surprised that his defender was none other than the father of the man he had killed. Trembling, he fell on his knees and pleaded, 'Dakheelek, dakheelek, ya saidi'. Torn between his love for his only son and the rage he felt against this young man, he paused in disbelief of the reality of what he had seen and heard. Finally, he answered, 'Allah demands that I protect you with all my means, even with my own life. Fear not, I shall.' Eventually the repentant young man, who greatly honored his noble benefactor and spared no effort to show it, received the most astonishing gift he could imagine. The landowner having proved his loyalty and trustworthiness told him, 'You left me without a son. Will you be my adopted son now?' What a happy end!

The Arabs were not ruthless, greedy oppressors. They fought to defend their tribes and tribal boundaries. But any innate lust for money and power was cultured by the unscrupulous examples of the oil companies. Instead of appealing to Islam's noble principles, which taught them to distribute national wealth for the welfare of the people, they inspired the sheiks to hoard the oil benefits or to spend them ridiculously on super-luxury travel, real estate, fine racing horses, and sports cars. What happened to the Koranic injunctions?

But this is the year 2000, another time, another opportunity. What if America could, in the interest of free enterprise, let OPEC set the oil price as high as it can. If prices were to get too high, we could let them sell the oil to whoever would want it, but we could set a limit on what we would pay. Furthermore, we could cease hoarding our own oil and work at decreasing our dependency.

What if Britain had never promised the Arabs independence from the Mediterranean to the Persian Gulf? It is conceivable that the Arabs would have continued to make room for the persecuted Jewish immigrants, as they had already done from 1880 until 1936 – that is until the combined efforts of the Balfour Declaration and Zionist ideologies became unendurable and the Arab perception of their right to independence clashed with the Zionist claims of ownership by divine decree. Perhaps had the Arabs never been given hope, they would not have developed such nationalism to defend their perceived right.

What if there had never been a Zionist Movement? Would it not have been possible, even probable, that returning Jews finding non-hostile Arabs would have entered the land without fear. They would have had no need to greet their hosts with the unpalatable assertion, 'We are coming back now. This land is ours, so you need to think about accepting our takeover'. The Jews are extremely sensitive to suffering people when their own sensitivities are not seared by political fires. Through their science and technology they have developed agriculture, irrigation, and land restoration skills far beyond the expectations of a country so small. They have shared what they have discovered with various nations around the world. It is unfortunate that their knowledge and generosity have been greatly hindered by the exorbitant expense of hostilities and the need to maintain a constant alert.

What if Israel had accepted God's timing, as the ultra-Orthodox Jews have been in favor of doing, by using all the possibilities at their disposal, unhindered by Zionist ideologies or by war for survival, while they waited for the fulfilling of prophecies? What if Israel could fully embrace the Messianic hope and distinctions, which her prophets foretold? What if the record of the Lord's interventions, which went to the point of making the sun stand still in its orbit for about a day or turning the clock back about ten minutes for Hezekiah, could convince her that Messiah can do or undo in a day far more than all her own harnessed nerve and sinew can accomplish from now until He comes? What if Israel could believe that, in order to make room for His glorious reign, the Seed of Abraham and Seed of David will have to sweep away all that she is so aggressively building up? The prophets foretold of earthquakes that will level the mountains and open a river from the Temple Mount to the Dead Sea – a river that will water the area and bring healing to the land on the east and shall flow into the Mediterranean on the west. What a relief for the water shortage! Zechariah 14.48 says,

> And his feet shall stand in that day upon the Mount of Olives, which is before Jerusalem on the east, and the Mount of Olives shall cleave in its midst toward the east and towards the west, and there shall be a very great valley; and half of the mountain shall remove toward the north and half of it shall remove toward the south ... And it shall be in that day that living waters shall go out from Jerusalem; half of them toward the former sea, and half of them towards the hinder sea; in summer and winter shall it be.

In His time the Messiah of Israel will change the whole topography of the land and bring healing and peace. What kind of peace? It will not be shaky human agreements, but according to Isa. 11.6,

> The wolf also shall dwell with the lamb, and the leopard shall lie down with the kid, and the calf and the young lion and the fatling together, and a little child shall lead them.

And Isa. 19.23-25 says,

> In that day shall there be a highway out of Egypt to Assyria and the Assyrian shall come into Egypt, and the Egyptian into Assyria and the Egyptians shall serve with the Assyrians.

In that day shall Israel be the third with Egypt and Assyria, even a blessing in the midst of the land; Whom the Lord of hosts shall bless, saying, 'Blessed be Egypt my people, and Assyria the work of my hands, and Israel mine inheritance.'

What if Israel could believe it, receive it? What if the Christian church had focused enough on the Lord Jesus Christ and listened to Him and made His last command the all consuming ministry of the church? The church could have then been more aware that Christians have been persecuted and martyred in this time more than in any other age. What will the answer be to the Lord's indictment recorded in Mt. 25:42-43, 45b?

For I was hungry, and ye gave me no food; I was thirsty, and ye gave me no drink; I was a stranger, and ye took me not in; naked, and ye clothed me not; sick, and in prison, and ye visited me not ... Inasmuch as ye did it not to one of the least of these, ye did it not unto me.

The Apostle Paul wrote in Gal. 6.10,

As we have, therefore, opportunity let us do good unto all men, especially unto them who are of the household of faith.

The world, except for some charitable societies, is not standing in line for the chance to rescue the dying Christians. Jesus cares that His body is being persecuted. He has provided His church with wealth, knowledge, and technological opportunities to intervene. In my opinion, the greatest opportunity for carrying out the Great Commission is for the peoples of the world to see the church humble itself and reach out and down to some of 'the least of these' their brethren and rescue them. That would give the church a credible voice, a certain validity that it currently just does not have in the eyes of the nations, tongues, and peoples who see little witness from the church of the passion of her Lord.

What if the prophetic interpreters of today were to realize that for Christians the Temple Mount has no great significance, as it relates, to the church age? The overpowering purpose for continuing focus on Mount Moriah in the Old Testament was because of a certain connection with Abraham that God had to satisfy. What did it have to do with Abraham? The story is told in Gen. 22.1-2:

> And it came to pass after these things, that God did test Abraham, and said unto him, 'Abraham,' and he said, 'Behold, here I am.' And he said, 'Take now thy son, thine only son Isaac, whom thou lovest, and get thee into the land of Moriah; and offer him there for a burnt offering upon one of the mountains which I will tell thee of.'

The very next morning, without divulging his assignment to anyone, he took Isaac, two servants, and the provisions for the sacrifice and started the trip. From Beersheba, where Abraham lived, it was a three-day trek to Jerusalem. On his journey, Abraham passed many mountains higher than Moriah, but since God had specifically said that He would show Abraham the right one, the patriarch watched and listened for the divine confirmation. The whole agonizing event no doubt tore at Abraham's heart until the moment, with knife ready to cut Isaac's throat, God stopped him. The ram was provided and Isaac was spared. Many more rams, lambs, and goats would be offered before the full meaning of the sacrifice would be revealed. I believe that God longed to reveal to Abraham what it was all about in that moment, but it was too far away and Abraham was too human to grasp the object lesson. God could have said, 'Abraham you will certainly offer your son on this selfsame mountain. Not Isaac, he will be your son and my only Son. We are in this together. I do not ask of you anything I do not plan to do, but on this very mountain your son and mine will give His life to open a fountain for cleansing for the whole world.'

Jews do not yet believe in Him. But when He returns in power and great glory that will change. According to Zech. 12.10 and 13.1,

> And I will pour upon the house of David, and upon the inhabitants of Jerusalem, the Spirit of grace and of supplications; and they shall look upon me whom they have pierced, and they shall mourn for him, as one mourneth for his only son, and shall be in bitterness for him as one that is in bitterness for his first born ... In that day there shall be a fountain

opened to the house of David and to the inhabitants of Jerusalem for sin and for uncleanness.

Considering that we all are guilty and need more than a ceremonial bath for cleansing, what if we could repent and join our voices in saying, 'Even so, come, Lord?'

7

SMALL ENOUGH TO STOP THE VIOLENCE

The numerous scenes of violence in Israel and the West Bank, such as the outbreak precipitated by Ariel Sharon's intrusion on the Temple Mount with the army behind him, have shocked every American. Any kind of war insults this nation's comfortable peace. All anyone knows to say is, 'Stop the violence!' From the people to the leaders, we just want the violence stopped, the disturbance to go away. The stone throwers are seen as inhuman, ruthless, out-of-control thugs who need to settle down so the peace talks can resume. America insists that Palestinian leaders can and must order the ruffians to settle down. No one seems to care that the revolt is nothing less than the death struggle of a despairing people. The whole convulsing calamity has brought me to respond with the question, 'Is there anyone small enough to stop the violence?' Many of the 'big', most powerful people of recent decades have tried to find a way to stop it. Actual peace negotiations have been going on longer than most thoughtful people believed they would be necessary. What caused the stalemate? Who is responsible for the gridlock? As I listen to Jim Lehrer, his commentators, the Secretary of State, and even the President himself, all I can hear are commands and questions. Nothing is new. No one reaches down to the core of the issues. Who can descend into the realities, and what can be done once they reach the bottom.

Certainly, the big political, religious, and cultural giants are too bloated by their knowledge, achievement, and position to fit into the narrow shaft of descent into the depths. It would take someone small enough to go through the 'needles-eye', someone who has nothing to lose, someone who is not afraid to be absolutely nothing and take the risks, assuming responsibilities of collective errors and admitting them, if not apologizing. Is there such a one?

History cannot be rewritten. Bad judgments and unwise choices of the past have carved indelible scars in the souls of the people. There are consequences for all actions and reactions, and the world cannot cover them up or demand them to go away. Acknowledging that certain things should not have been said or done do little to ease the pain, to cool tempers, to provide a basis to end violence, and to make peace, unless there is someone humble enough to inspire mutual confessions of wrongdoing by one's own example of vulnerability and to ask God to take control.

German leaders who had nothing to do with the Holocaust had to apologize for the atrocities of the Nazi regime. All of the compassion of the restored Germany combined with fifty years of paying reparations could not reach into the depths of the crushed spirits of the Holocaust survivors to sound a grace note capable of healing the broken chords and restoring the lost melody.

President Clinton was courageous enough to pull back the curtain from the poorly concealed sins of the United States against the Japanese Americans committed during World War II and ask forgiveness for the nation. He also apologized to black Americans for the inhumanities this 'Christian' nation has committed against them. Yet, it does not yet appear that our leaders realize that America committed political, cultural, and religious errors against the Arabs and the Jews, causing repercussions that cannot be stayed without divine intervention. Have our leaders ever entertained the thought that with God all things are possible? Matthew 19.24, 26 says,

> And again I say unto you, 'It is easier for a camel to go through the eye of a needle than for a rich man to enter the kingdom of God' … But Jesus beheld them and said unto them, 'With men this is impossible but with God all things are possible.'

The struggling people are rich in anger, self-justification, and resentment, to which they cling – remnants of the cruel, fearful words and deeds exchanged. What stripped-down person can encourage both sides to lay aside their burdens and grievances, confess their own wrong doings, and ask God to show them the way to go on from here in peace.

I just simply cannot believe it! Today while I prepared to write this chapter, I stopped to hear the news of the election results. Instead of learning who is the next president, I heard a most extraordinary proposition that closely resembles the idea of being 'small enough to stop the violence'. On the News Hour with Jim Lehrer, the possibility was advanced that both candidates, Governor George Bush and Vice-President Al Gore, have a unique chance at a great prize. One, either one, could immortalize his political stature by conceding the victory to the other. The other one would become president of the United States.

The numerous reasons why it is most unlikely to find a 'taker of the great prize' make the mere suggestion seem ludicrous. But is it?

Human beings cling to power as to life itself. Yet there comes a point when the suffering is too great and the strength fails so drastically that one relinquishes even life. As difficult as that passage is, the dying one can have hope beyond life. Most religions believe there waits a better life beyond this one.

Dying in order to live is not a new idea; it is the basis of life. A seed dies that it may germinate and reproduce itself many times over. A caterpillar spins its cocoon tomb around itself and ceases to exist in its original form. Science cannot unravel the life process at work in the 'dead seed' or in the petrified larva. But that is not the end. In the fullness of time, dictated by each individual DNA, a plant sprouts or butterfly emerges. Life is full of such analogies. Why, then, is the earlier suggestion so inconceivable? Why is it hard to believe that something good can come out of the ashes of personal humiliation? It is not only believable; it is inevitable. Magnanimity of spirit, when it is pure, free from pride, bitterness, or retaliations, cannot die. It returns a nobler life, full of promise for higher purpose and productivity.

It is just such a call that breaks forth from this present moment – a call for some person or group of persons to rise to the occasion for the Middle East. If such a one were to appear as a 'humble, honest broker', apologizing for all the sins of the Western governments, churches, and ideologies that have helped to produce the present chaos, it could form a basis for what could be some surprising and seminal discussions and negotiations. The very surprise could stop the violence and restore hope that at least there is something to talk about. There can be a new beginning.

Photographs

Margaret Gaines
Founder and Principal of Aboud School 1970-83

Arlene Miller
Principal of Aboud School 1983-93

Margaret in native Palestinian garb

Original Church building constructed 1969

Aboud Elementary School, Kindergarten, and Church Ministries Building

Dedication of original school building

Margaret cutting the ribbon at the dedication

Carrying food to guests during dedication

Present day Church and Parsonage in Aboud

Kindergarten constructed 1997

Morning assembly

Children on the playground

Aboud's School Teachers

Sunday School Palm Sunday March

In the classroom

Margaret and Zarefie

Aboud Church Congregation

Index of Biblical References

Made in the USA
Middletown, DE
15 January 2018